Social Media

The Sum of Everything Equals Zero

A Guide to the

Rational Facts Surrounding

A Virtual World on the

Human Condition

Written by Alastair R Agutter

English Language

BOOK COVER DESIGN:

By Alastair R Agutter

ORIGINAL ARTWORK AND IMAGES

By Alastair R Agutter

AUTHOR WEB SITE

www.alastairagutter.com

PUBLISHED BY

Create Space Independent Publishing

An Amazon Group Company

First Edition Published: 24th February 2016

ISBN-10: 1518716679

ISBN-13: 978-1518716676

Table of Contents

Preface

Since having been involved with the World Wide Web since it's commercial beginning back in the mid 1990's, as a Computer Scientist and Program Developer.

I like to think I can offer some clear water, regarding such a phenomena we know as Social Media today, and where even in a Virtual World, the real physical presence of Sir Isaac Newton's Natural Law is evident, and using both Quantum Mechanics and Natural Branching, even in an Artificial Intelligence environment, as written about in my book titled Creating the New Internet Super Highway.

So this new realm is not for the complacent or faint hearted. As further evidence of this power today has been with the Weaponization of Social Media."

Introduction

The first question many would ask is "why write this book?"

Well the truth is, in this fast changing and frenetic World of technology, even as an architect navigating and exploring greater advancements looking into the future, I have to also declare myself to be a bit of a Dinosaur to a degree, regarding values and morality!

I am often described by close friends as living in the wrong time. For I believe in human "truth and values," a commodity less freely given and in great decline these days. Such an example of the decline of moral standards is present in the current and no doubt future Politicians, Prime Ministers and Presidents.

Also from studying Sir Isaac Newton's Natural Law and the World of Quantum Mechanics that is still a puzzlement to many Scientists and Biologists today it serves me well as all does make absolute sense and why I do exist in this timeline of the human story, to offer balance!

I wanted to write this book therefore to give some truthful answers and balance to the phenomena of Social Media and real power, as it is having an impact on society in many forms.

The virtual world of Social Media is now having a significant effect on society, the human condition and world around us, yet many are unaware or still do not really grasp the environment and ramifications.

I have broken the book down into relevant sections of interest for all Social Media players, be it as users or for commercial operatives. So they can draw from each topic, valuable information concerning the respective related areas.

"We all need to understand and appreciate the role and importance of technology, where it is there to assist, not to make us dependent."

Alastair R Agutter

Social Media Roots

I often hear folk say, especially across Social Media Networks that they "live for today and never look at the past." Well as I said, I am always very honest and you will find this throughout the book, but as a frank positive!

Therefore relating to the above comment and statement so often spoken today, it should be consigned to the World of fools. Every aspect of evolution and invention goes through processes of change. By recording and understanding the history of such events, can you then change and improve, be it society or a product invention.

So regarding the roots of Social Media these facts are very important, as they record the evolution of the beast and will therefore as a result help assistance us, in understanding the future cycles and changes that can be expected!

There were essentially three components relating to the early roots of Social Media and Networking.

These were and are:-

1/. Chat

2/. Free Web Space

3/. Web Forums

1/. Chat

The first component "chat" became available on early operating systems such as Windows 98 and Windows NT4. Chat also

7

became available on browser suite bundles from Netscape in the form of "AOL Instant Messenger (AIM)" and via the main portal web site. Any fan of the fabulous movie "You've Got Mail" starring Tom Hanks and Meg Ryan, would see how the movie captures those early days of social networking.

To try and help capture those early periods of development leading to Social Media, the following image shows a "Classic Netscape Browser" with a Netscape 1998 Netcenter News web page that I archived for historic importance and prosperity. Access to the application and function of the Instant Messenger service, was enabled by using the Netscape browser's Window tab at the top of the program suite.

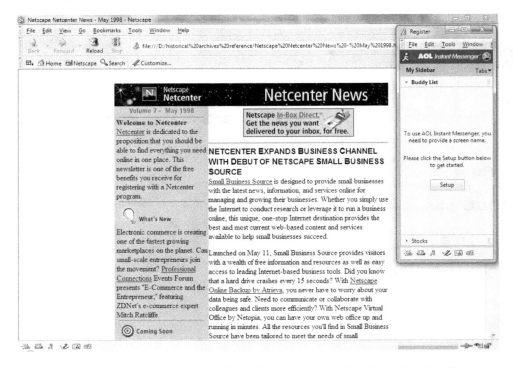

Back to 1998: Photograph and Digital image created by Alastair R Agutter

It may come as a surprise to many, but still today the AIM or AOL Instant Messaging service still continues at the time of publishing this book in February 2016.

2/. Free Web Space

In the late 90's another component to the eventual birth of Social Media as we know it today, was the availability of "Free" web space for the consumer user or webmaster enthusiast from Yahoo known as "Geocities" and Lycos known as "Tripod" to mention just two, where anyone could sign up and get free web space, to promote or write about anything they wanted.

However this is where it gets interesting, for you often hear in the News and Media the coined phrase the "World Wild West" and this is simply not true!

From the very beginning of the commercial World Wide Web as I call it dating from 1995, there has always been ethical standards and protocols. It may come as a surprise again to many, but today these protocols still exist with the big players and the most respected in the industry concerning the World Wide Web.

The free web space of the day back in the late 90's was often frowned upon, as part of the free web space agreement was to allow the host, this being Yahoo for Geocities and Lycos for Tripod, to display advertising in the form of 468 x 60 pixel banner adverts. These were normally positioned towards the top or at the bottom of these free web pages.

3/. Forums

Web forums often known as news posts, was the third component regarding the eventual rise of Social Media as we know it today! At these venues, members of the web user community could interact with webmasters by placing messages and posts onto articles or features they read. They were also venues to leave comments that were moderated by the webmaster owner of the particular web site in question.

These three components were and are the foundation of most if not all Social Media Networks today. In reality the changes and appearance to these programs and applications today, is as a result of clever marketing and bundling up.

The terminology of "Social Media" as opposed to "free web space, chat and forums" does sound sexy admittedly, but under the hood in reality terms, today the terminology of "Web 2.0" and "Social Media Networks" are what Sir Tim Berner's-Lee and myself, describe as jargon based!

What is clear from looking at the emergence of Social Media as we know it today, as opposed to the early days of the web with these component technologies in place, we will find that the only difference being the marketability of the concept!

Social Media Networks is a far smarter marketing terminology as a brand to reach the masses as opposed to being a Webmaster.

The environment of "free" web space in those early days compared to "free" social media web space today and is in reality terms not very different in a commercial sense.

So often what we understand to be new technology today can be found in component form from the past.

Another good and fine example today of marketing and bundling up a technology to look sexy is "Cloud Storage" or "the Cloud" which is simply web hosting storage.

However, there is still on very rare occasion's today great opportunity in technology services online for the very many mindless idiot investors who know nothing about the industry currently backing the wrong horse as they say!

The Phenomena

The phenomena of Social Media cannot be denied, Facebook today boasts over a billion users and again this relates to understanding the key success here being "marketability" regarding user take up!

As like throughout history and today, somewhere in the equation of human advancement has come with it to succeed as a product or service the talents of a "salesman."

Again in history this can be seen regarding the early days of the Video recorder surrounding Betamax and VHS. The latter succeeded through better marketing. However the greater lose to humanity in the form of advancement was Betamax, a far better technology and as a result of commercialism prevailing over technology. Beta programming and development therefore had only really finally started to evolve some 20 to 30 years later. Today virtually every new technology devised or created has the gene code of Betamax somewhere embedded.

The World Wide Web and the phenomena of Social Media Networks is a sales concept we have often seen throughout society and in commercialism especially in the form of clothing design that we describe and know today as "fashion" or "trends" and the latter word especially resonates with the World Wide Web and Social Media, when we often see "trending" as a word to indicate popularity of an event or subject that is of interest to the masses.

By understanding the landscape of change we can see here with Social Media Networks on the World Wide Web in the commercial sense, how it has also adopted many proven existing elements of the past such as fashion and trends as commercial vehicle components.

The phenomena and dynamic concept of Social Media therefore has to be appreciated as none other than a commercialized vehicle grabbing elements that work. For it has been clearly demonstrated and established above that the components in the way of fashion and trends have now been migrated and deployed to the World Wide Web today in the guise of Social Media, forming a commercial environment and where some would rightly say mediocrity, especially if we take another element example from society, this being local gossip!

So then again by studying the history and landscape of the environment surrounding the World Wide Web today and Social Media Networks, we can quickly agree from the evidence we see, what comes next with fashion and trends for example is further change, but of a more superficial nature!

A woman's skirt for example can be designed and altered in many ways, but at the end of the day it is still a skirt.

The emergence of Apps (applications) today as a bolt on technology is again a programming method that was used in the mid to late 90's with regards to the World Wide Web. But again today, such a technology has been aptly described and dressed up to be something else and more dynamic.

Again Apps as a success is as a result of good salesmanship and in our industry when it came to marketing, there was none better than the late Steve Jobs.

Today the Apple brand in the way of Computing excels today as a result of marketing ability and kudos. This I fully understand in many ways when I have developed great luxury sporting goods in the past that were far superior than anything else on the Market. This can be said for Microsoft and the reasons why I still use

Windows today as an operating system; for the sheer simple fact and truth is the Microsoft product is far better than Apple's, but the Apple marketing machine has prevailed in this instant as did VHS over Betamax surrounding the Video Recorder!

Social Media as a marketing phenomenon for which it is, has become a monster in the form of commercial opportunity. Especially in the servicing sector, namely capitalism and money! However, as demonstrated above surrounding the history of Betamax verses VHS, not all commercial trends or traits are necessarily conducive for long term sustainability success in the form of human advancement and the environment.

The success from Social Media today has been engrained into a society as a trend and habit of "can do and must use" regardless of content or consequence.

As a result of such facts explained above, surrounding Social Media society demand, there will always be fallout with the introduction of any new product or service. The best and most truthful answer and example I can give, is the creation of alcohol and what comes with that in the way of fall out is alcoholism, broken lives and mental illness.

Today in our society we all accept that we live in a global world, therefore the impact of any new creation or offering is international and reaching every part of the world. So there is a great burden of responsibility on the shoulders of all citizen users and especially technology developers today, as there is now international consequence.

If I was in Montana developing an electrical plant and accidently blew the thing up from my endeavours and experiment, it would only impact the local community at worse!

14

The World Wide Web today and the International community is a completely different animal as they say!

By reaching such a point in technology in many respects can be a good indicator to establish where Social Media Networking is on the human evolutionary timeline and by studying the history of such a phenomena, it enables us to establish where we are and have reached when creations are now being dressed up, this must therefore surely demonstrate that a peak point of saturation has arrived and been reached.

Towards the end of last year and at the beginning of this year among circles, I have been frequently hearing people ask about what is the next big thing!

Well this is an interesting question and the answer in truth is far less glamourous than one would hope and both history across many fields and advancements including the historical geographical landscape changes of the World Wide Web spells out an answer of "maintenance," or in the big league due to product and service saturation "mergers and acquisitions" that are starting to happen now.

In the days of the "Wild West," any interloper arriving on your patch in those days would of led to a show down or shoot out, as only one could exist.

In 1999 to 2000 we saw the Dot.Com crash, as a result of the human trait being, to follow a trend and where many were investing in things they knew absolutely nothing about.

So the phenomena of Social Media internationally has a great burden of consequence in the way of direction and standards and this is why the word "maintenance" is key, for if we have cycled up

15

to a saturation point or peaked, as often described, this means to maintain and keep an audience, the service offered has to be one of quality for the viewer and user.

The other big question with regards to the Social Media user is "what's in it for them," and how do they benefit or gain!

The reality of the Social Media phenomena was as a result of chat, forums and free web being bundled up to appear as an easy universal standard that was accessible to all. It did in many respects transform a world of humans into enthusiast computer geeks!

One thing about the human condition and especially surrounding Men is the refusal to ask, especially when one doesn't know something and so as these Social Media Networks opened and grew, there were countless tens of thousands of new users attaining greater computer literate skills from learning about the Social Media platform.

For the masses, what was in it for them was a venue of Social Media existence to say to the World "look" I exist!

As these platforms evolved and incorporated more features by bringing the audience along with them. Photo libraries soon become commercial considerations with opportunity in the form of product release images etc. And like forums, a venue to leave feedback creating greater interaction between the product user and other potential customers and followers, created greater opportunity and engagement and this was especially a benefit to the commercial world.

The emergence of the Social Media phenomena also brings with it social ills in the form of voyeurism, jealousy and abuse. These latter traits reflect on all of society and especially with an online Social Media Network platform, where such traits and habits can propagate very quickly like a virus.

Very often impulse moments can have long and devastating consequences to the brand or a victim individual. This aptly demonstrates the nature of the beast regarding the burden of responsibility and a fine line, as successful advertising campaigns are mostly based on the emotion of users or viewers.

After the initial fervour of "hey I am here" with the posting of images and interacting with some friends and family. You then have to ask the question again "what's in it for them" and here one or two things will happen!

It is a given that the landscape of the World Wide Web and the World of Social Media Networks will be changing and in this equation is money and users!

In a commercial environment regarding the capitalist beasts they need to make money for their shareholders and so it is imperative to "maintain" interest and demand.

To make money for their shareholders they have to retain and try to grow their audience base.

In every equation and outcome there will be casualties as a result of change. History has demonstrated this regarding even the commercial World Wide Web as I call it and none more so than the early period that saw the "Browser Wars" between Netscape and Microsoft!

Many would think today that Facebook is impervious to demise, but understanding history of the World Wide Web and the technology sector, Facebook believe it or not, is one of the most vulnerable!

A good example is surrounding the browser Wars where Netscape commanded 93% of all the World's online users, but lost to Microsoft with Internet Explorer!

As we go through this book you will see the fall out already surrounding Social Media Networks and where there will be many losers and very few winners!

There is a rule often applied in Business and Marketing known as the 80/20 rule. In the World of technology the percentage ratios are far greater and more ruthless, I coined as the 94/6 rule!

Branding and Image

Socrates once said "the greatest form of evil is ignorance or the pretence of knowing" and this in many respects relates to the lack of understanding surrounding brands and the association with Social Media Networks!

You can also apply the 94/6 rule regarding the complete understanding of Social Media and so any member of the community reading, needs not to be too alarmed for when you are dealing with technology, the reality is behind such creations are many of the greatest minds known to man today Internationally.

The best analogy I can give is that you are no longer playing in the local village non-league football team, but now in the World Cup and fighting for your lives to win!

The other fact you need to know and can draw from regarding this sector to make you feel much better if you are tipping your toes into the World of Social Media for the first time, even the likes of CNN, BBC, Fords and countless other World Business players do not get it!

So what are the facts and gravity of "Branding and Image" surrounding Social Media?

Well here again I will be truthful in this book and you may describe my work like "Marmite," you either like it, or hate it and in many respects this is most apt based on Facebook's like buttons!

You will either like it for the book's truthful honesty and facts to help. Or hate it, as a result of refusing to accept the reality of Social Media as a "Virtual World" with regards to understanding.

Either way, whether you like this book or hate it, does not trouble me, for the path for greater enlightenment and to be in God's favour is through love, truth and sincerity!

Branding and image starts with a tangible item or service and found within these items, products or services is the value offered.

The value of an item product or service is based on the investment made by the brand owner or brand's enterprise. Again this can and does relate to the history of the item, product or service often described as provenance.

So if we take Social Media as a Brand service initially, how would we determine its value?

Can we describe Social Media as an exclusive high end product or service, no is the answer. Can we describe Social Media as a middle of the road type of product or service, the answer again here is no!

The reason why we are unable to really quantify Social Media is for the fact it is what it is!

Social Media for a brand venue, product, item or service is used by all and in all its diversity of users.

When I use to market our luxury handcrafted Gaming Sports Split Bamboo Fly Rods costing in excess of a £1,000 ($1,500) over 30 years ago, they would be advertised in magazines such as "The Field" or "Field and Stream" for example. They would certainly not be advertised in the "Exchange and Mart" for the simple reason of damaging the Brand!

So when I see leading luxury brands promoting themselves via Facebook in truth I cringe, as I do know the long term ramifications with regards to damaging the brand!

Many businesses today are clueless when it comes to Social Media Networking, as I see so many gleefully boasting and asking users to visit and see them on "Facebook" these including brands across the spectrum be it luxury goods or cheap plastic junk as I call it!

With regards to luxury brands and Facebook, it's like contacting all your valuable clients and asking them to meet you down at the local Car Boot Sale. Instead of giving clients a VIP invite to the Game Fair at Chatsworth and knowing a degree of obligation will be felt to buy something at such an exclusive and famous venue! This in turn creating greater sales and brand awareness.

In the 1980's I was invited to help a Company launch a new Graphite product in the Tennis Sports Industry and as it was a new invention and up market, I made arrangements to meet up with a much respected colleague Gerald Holmes of Holmes and Marchant Plc the big Pharmaceutical industry players, as Gerald had a top leading successful marketing and advertising agency known as "Blitz" in London. It was a given the new product would be advertised in all the leading publications including Harpers and the LTA magazine. At no time would we ever dream of advertising in one of the more generalized sports publications or newspapers. The sheer fact being the development and protection of the brand!

Whilst enjoying a summer afternoon with Gerald at his Family retreat in High Wycombe in England, we discussed name association branding as a new concept in those days and looked at the Sports Industry especially, regarding again the outfall and loss of credibility in the Banking, Finance and Insurance industry sector.

21

Again the banks had gone back to their bad old ways, investing and speculating in crap and where many went bust later including Midland Bank Plc. In those days Banks and Insurance Companies had to regain the trust of the public and customers and so they started to sponsor sporting events to be part of society again. The guy down the street being a lover of Football was more inclined now to open a building society account with the Nationwide as they were sponsoring for example the England National Football Team. Another example was National Westminster Bank moving into Cricket and sponsoring the "one-days" and eventually leagues etc.

Developing and building any brand takes many years of hard graft and thought. Yet when it comes to Social Media, all the rules of consequence and responsibility to protect the legacy of the brand appears to be thrown out of the window why?

The simple truth and fact is most in Business, do not understand Social Media and the implications!

If you have a really fabulous product and brand built up over many years, like James Purdey & Sons "Best London Guns" as a result of family generations and craftsmanship, what message are you sending to countless generations of existing and potentially new clients, if you are promoting or associating the brand with the likes of Facebook?

The simple answer to the above is the absolute destruction to the brand and its kudos in the World. But the ramifications are even greater as there are political and social consequences. For as a Social Media environment and venue like Facebook, there are all sorts of controversial activities and opinions including the darkest aspects of society in the form of paedophilia, extremism and child abuse to mention a few!

22

So you do have to ask yourself as a Business owner of a brand what the hell are you doing! The invite to the client to see "your business" on Facebook destroys the image of the brand in their eyes and demonstrates mindless acts of desperation.

There are without doubt plenty of experts out there in the World regarding Social Media, but in reality are clueless and dangerous. This then takes us back to that word of consequence!

The sad reflection on society today is that the environment is becoming forever more superficial and enterprises are now very easily getting caught up in this nonsense, for fear of losing out, or not keeping up with the times of change.

But the reality is throughout life and history, including the cosmos, there are constants. The Sun will rise in the East and set in the West that is a fact and will not change. Social Media or any other form of man-made product or service will not change these events and constant cycles of evolution regardless.

Brands can change and move with the times but with balanced reasoning and understanding. Sadly, when it comes to Social Media most do not understand!

There is also the risk of brand and image exposure to unwanted negative responses. As a result of ill thought out Social Media Marketing in such an environment of diversity, where brands can receive negative comments and this can cause great impact to the products and brand simply, for the fact that someone is jealous of success, or has a resentment towards a product, simply for the fact that they cannot afford it, and this can have a significant and long lasting damaging effect on any business.

Now some so called experts may say this is good, but these are the same people that just talk and write about a subject suffering from verbal diarrhoea and produce nothing tangible.

There is nothing wrong in being transparent and accountable as a Business, in fact it is a very good thing regarding the evolutionary changes that need to take place across society including "New Era Enterprise" that I wrote about nearly 10 years ago and the need for these new businesses to emerge and co-exist in concert at the heart of communities.

But the reality is at the end of the day, there has to be a framework of some form to avoid chaos, and the rule of Natural Law throughout the Cosmos is evident and also down here on Earth with the new RDFa (HTML 5.0) framework standard created by the World Wide Web Consortium (W3C) with regards to the net!

The environment of Social Media Networking across many platforms is simply suicidal to many brands and services, as a result of Senior Management or staff incumbents involved in these activities failing to understand, or read the landscape and what seems to be a generational loss in brand marketing skills, where businesses are becoming forever exposed on a daily basis.

So as a brand or product, where image matters and where it does for all businesses, risk aversion needs to be applied with some great thought. Any environment that you are associated with and where you have no influence or control over is not good to say the least!

Brand and image awareness is a key mechanism for success and there are many other more productive forms of marketing that can be applied for a greater reception and respect for the brand, image and the historical legacy of the Business.

Now some may say this is not always relevant to every business, but I say it is for whoever founded such an enterprise, there is very often a dedicated marriage of love and heart ache!

One of the oldest sayings in Business is "it takes many years to acquire a good name in business and easy to get a bad name overnight" and such sentiments are still pertinent today.

I no longer make luxury sporting goods for commercial gain, for as like brands such as Aston Martin, Lotus and others, you can very often become easily tired and weary of the philistines that surround you, namely bankers who have no appreciation of worth as valuable contributions to culture and society. One of my greatest regrets was being forced to sell one of my businesses from a lack of bank vision and funding, only to see the legacy and brand be destroyed from short term vision and desire for quick profit!

As we go through the book some of the questions you may now be asking, will be answered surrounding Marketing and Presence, to protect brand and image to ensure long term success!

Marketing and Money

Any good top flight marketing person will echo my comments in this Chapter, and the answers found online from the so called experts offering services for a few dollars, is a complete waste of valuable web space and time!

The first thing any person should know as a consumer, going into business for one's self, it is very rarely about profit. It is very often as a result of a need or opportunity and why products and services come to be.

The famous Co-Operatives founded in history were as a result of the need for fair priced food and product availability in community regions.

Speaking from experience, when I first went into business, it was to make the best products at all costs in the luxury sporting goods sector and the business became a family member with a soul, as the brand and products came to life from my design drawings.

A brand and image meant something in times gone bye, it was your signature in the World in a way in which to contribute to help in the human advancement story.

It was a journey of great heart ache, trial and error when products were being developed with countless hours never recorded in monetary terms. History is a testament to these words and sentiments as we look at the many marvels that have shaped our World today and the dedicated players who we still acknowledge today such as Tesla, Edison, Marconi, Bush, Hertz, Whittle, Mitchell, Rolls and Royce to mention a few.

I remember a saying once as we discuss Marketing and Money here, where it was once said "you can have the best product in the world, but if nobody knows about it, you won't sell any" and this is what it's about at the end of the day after the product creation, it then comes down to the marketing.

So with a great product and brand how can Social Media serve to create awareness in the World for your fabulous products and services?

Well in truth, we may have lightly covered the Facebook scenario earlier regarding name association and invites, that is the equivalent of an invitation to a boot sale and this is a fact. You only have to look at the Facebook platform in its true form beyond the hype, to realize it is a media venue for the personal user compiled from Chat, Forum and Free Web Space Software, nothing more!

Facebook also comes with other baggage as mentioned earlier, surrounding the wilful negligence of material published on the platform and where none of which would any self-respecting business seek to be associated with.

There is another old saying "you can fool some of the people some of the time, but you cannot fool all of the people all of the time" and eventually I hope folk will eventually see through Facebook, only as a machine and vehicle for opportunist owners and shareholders to make money and nothing else. It certainly does not serve the interests of the consumer or the business enterprise and this will be covered later in the Chapters for Human Health and Facebook.

I see many invites by businesses with Facebook pages and in truth, I will tell you what goes through my mind regarding this activity and the image these folk are portraying to the World regarding their business and brand.

Facebook Invite by a Business my thoughts are: - "Oh dear, how sad, they can't be serious, cannot even afford their own web site, and must be dodgy, possibly another scam.

You see history again here provides an insight and relevance to the geographical landscape changes and its importance, for when the web began to get going in a commercial sense back in the middle to late 90's. The way to get out the "Word" about your business existence to the rest of the world was in the form of marketing online through Search Engines.

The ones of the day back in the 90's regarded as the main players are as follows.

Search Engines of the Day!

1/. Yahoo

2/. MSN

3/. AltaVista

4/. Mamma

5/. Excite

6/. Lycos

7/. Dog Pile

8/ Hotbot

9/. Search

10/. Dmoz

11/. AllTheWeb

12/. Web Spider

Today being in charge of your own destiny as an enterprise and for protecting your brand and image still requires first and foremost search engines.

Many of the names above have now gone, or been taken over in a "maintenance" (consolidation and acquisitions) period post the Dot.Com crash and in many respects from the emergence of only a few major players today, namely Google and Bing (yahoo). This helps enterprise to direct energy and find synergy from these few search engines remaining and from the very outset, business owners (webmasters) should be building a positive relationship with these search engines, by researching and taking the time to ensure that the businesses information to promote their Company and Brand via the Search Engine is spider friendly, when these search engines are data mining, gathering information.

Two years ago, I wrote a book titled "Getting Inside Google's Head" and it was specifically written for business owners and in plain English, drilling down on the key components elements required from a web site and the web pages, especially under the hood as they say, regarding meta data!

Nothing surprises me here, but whilst the book sells a considerable number of copies each year, it pales in comparison to the number of web sites on the net ran by businesses. The great tragedy here in many respects, demonstrates the habits and behavioural patterns of the current society regarding cultural human activity of believing to "know" and failing to take the time to understand and research the environment. But instead again, taking advice from parts of the web that can only deliver very generalized, misleading, or superficial waffle!

The hard facts and reality regarding your brand and products on the World Wide Web, is that you need a major presence on Search Engines. For if you have no literature in hard copy form and do not have any retail outlets known to all in the communities at large world-wide, you will be dependent on the web to which your business will live or die from successful search engine marketing and placement results.

By investing into an online presence working with major search engines, will quickly bring success if carried out the correct way and so any business worth their sort, will need their very own web site. So then the business can be in charge of its own destiny and also very importantly, be able to present the brand and products in the correct way, with the constant brand theme being carried through across all spectrums of marketing and name association branding exercise as seen by Rolex, Cartier, Gucci and others.

Not having your own web site and just buying a domain name and linking it to the likes of Facebook, is what it is!

The harsh reality and facts are, you will never be taken seriously as a business brand, or as serious player, unless your operation is in fact a scam, or selling crap to the masses and driven solely by money and this methodology will certainly have no long term sustainability and will eventually lead to meeting the long arm of the law!

Keeping clear of marketing scams out on the web and across countless Social Media Networks can be difficult at times, as there are many opportunists out there offering to get 100's if not 1000's of customers to Social Media Network sites, with many varying prices and these are all scams in some form, generated by software programming and data bases.

Very sadly regarding Social Media, as like when the web really started to get going, rational thought seemed to go out of the window by business owners and senior managers. They saw the emergence of this new trend of the web like a Tsunami and believed without thinking, they just had to be on the top of this tidal movement and the value of the brand and business suddenly became a secondary consideration.

I have witnessed this first-hand, where at the beginning of commercial web as I describe it, when as a Director for Satellite and Cable Europe, we had clients asking for web sites, simply for the fact that "they suppose they better have one" and without any real thought as to the real evolutionary needs of the brand.

So it is very important to keep things in prospective, with reference to the affinity you have for your Business and Brand, after countless years of hard graft and heart ache, requires some rational thinking.

As a marketing professional or business owner, you need to start thinking about how you would go about "searching" out a product or service you wish to buy, this can be a good starting point, by putting yourself in the mind of your potential customers. Today almost 99% of the time, if you are a potential customer and do not have the brands domain name you seek to buy from a glossy magazine for example, your first port of call will be "Google" and that's a fact!

If you are looking for some fabulous furnishings, perfumes or a professional service, you certainly will not be going to a Social Media site such as Facebook will you!

So then you have to again rationally ask yourself what's the big deal about Social Media Networks, as your aim in business is to market and promote your great brand and the products to eventually make a profit (money) and so is Social Media Marketing on Facebook for example the answer.

As I said earlier, Social Media Networks are what they are! Many Businesses including the News and Media world do not have a clue on how to use these platforms for their own advantage. Instead News, Media, Businesses and users are in reality working for these Social Media Network sites and platforms.

The harsh facts are from clever marketing and hype, Social Media Networks are forever getting bigger and the businesses and brands in the community are becoming forever weaker, as they drive more traffic to the Social Media Network sites, rather than using them to drive traffic to their own web sites.

In the marketing scheme of things surrounding Social Media Networks, it is not wise either to directly use your Business or Brand on them, for many of the above reasons given earlier regarding content material published such as Child abuse and Extremism.

But there are ways to use Social Media Networks to drive more users to your business web site and without risking any association with them for the above reasons given and in earlier parts of the book.

You do not have to advertise on Social Media Networks, the likes of Facebook etc. As this money is wasted and you might as well set fire to the cash!

If we agree the likes of Facebook covers the masses and yes they do claim to be able to measure audiences to target advertise. Again you need to look at the bigger picture regarding the audience base. Why are folk using Facebook for example in the first place, what type of people are they!

The reality is regarding Facebook and other Social Media Networks is a vanity quest, whether you like to accept it or not. Most folk using such services are posting comments, views, opinions, personal experiences and photographs about themselves!

User activity in most cases on Social Media Networks is not related to the hunting out, or searching of products, unless it relates to a brand or company, that could already have negative baggage and the user wants to know more before they consider buying a product, or using a service from them.

The damage caused as mentioned earlier in the book, amounts to not being in charge of your own destiny as a business and allowing the brand to be exposed to such an environment. The problems created or caused will eventually lead back to the Business and Owner with long lasting effects.

Social Media Networks in many respects evolves around emotions, therefore a marketing environment created not for businesses or other organizations, but for Facebook itself to attract more users to then in turn perpetuate and generate more advertisement impressions to generate revenue for the owners and shareholders of Facebook.

If Facebook was focused on any honourable effort to link the World and create a new philosophical World for transparency and to shape a more equal World for all of society, it certainly would not of gone public as a Nasdaq Business.

When you start to look at the bigger picture, you can then get to see a clearer picture of the landscape before you.

You know if you enter the snake or lion's den you can expect to be bitten. This is why Facebook is vulnerable and will eventually fall like a pack of cards, as the World begins to see through the deceit to which the whole Facebook experience is. Facebook for example applies risk aversion and protection. It is not the free and easy laid back image the founder Mark Zuckerberg gives.

For I am sure now many users in business or discontent consumers have tried to get answers, or make contact with Facebook staff on matters that concern them, or in plain language need help! But the reality is, the responses you get are mostly automated and self-generated by technology programming.

Facebook say they take child abuse and extremism seriously, but this is not the case, for any self-respecting enterprise would allocate the required staff in numbers to bring down the offensive material. No effort is made to remove such material, only when it affects Facebook and reaches the World at large via News and Media!

Such facts are interesting, for it clearly demonstrates that any business should be in charge of its own destiny, for Facebook is and contrary to what is believed, does know of the damaging offensive material, but allows it to be published for the simple wicked cynical reasons of greater viewing numbers, that is then turned and converted into money based on the number of advertising page impression exposures.

So as a Business of any worth, you should be giving Facebook a very wide berth and so there is a massive expance of water between your business and Facebook. The furthest the better, for any name association with such an organization now and in the future will spell damage to your business and brand.

Facebook like other networks can be used as briefly mentioned in marketing, but this is done in a personal way by registering individuals onto the Social Media Network site in the form of trusted staff and where they can make posts saying how great a product is and why folk should visit the web site, this being the business web site, promoting your brand, promoting your products and services your way.

Instead of promoting Facebook, which every business is doing today by saying "hey come and link up, or join us on Facebook" oh please!

By using trusted staff and individuals to promote the Business via Facebook, it gives you that gap of protection as your Business name and brand is not directly related, or associated with the Social Media Network site.

In truth, if you are a Wedding Company of sorts and have a page on Facebook saying how great you are, do you really want your users to see sex toys being advertised as part of the Facebook money making advertising machine when you are selling a bridesmaids outfit.

Many Bloggers and Social Media Networkers get this form of marketing and in truth this is how they make their money, by posting countless products claiming they use them and saying how great they are with referral links from an affiliate program that they are a member of for a company, or many companies and where they receive a percentage commission on every sale.

I have to laugh about marketing regarding Social Media, for the most powerful Social Media Network with the greatest potential today for Business, News and Media is Twitter! Yet in recent days and weeks the money men (investors) in the Stock Markets are moving away from a service that has marvellous potential, as they do not get it, or understand the geographical landscape!

If I want to make the World aware of a new book like this one when published, I will use Twitter as one of my first ports of call for Twitter is what it is!

Twitter is a very powerful "News Feed Ticker" as I describe it and able to reach countless thousands and millions within minutes of launching a new product on "Your" web site, "NOT" Facebooks for example, to attract countless thousands of new visitors and potential customers.

From smart marketing, staff can post great product feeds all day long on Twitter at intervals, constantly attracting more visitors to your web site.

The benefits are immeasurable on Twitter, 1/ its "Free" and 2/ the visitors are genuinely interested in your products and they will invariably follow you, or place your links in a saved file known as a list, to buy products at a later date!

Making money online and promoting your brand in the right way first comes with search engines and having your web site geared up with the right information, so the Company Brand web site becomes search engine friendly when they are data mining, gathering your valuable product information. This will also ensure good placements in the search engine results, if you have taken the trouble to make sure the meta data and architecture is fundamentally right on your web site as covered in "Getting Inside

Google's Head Book" for the process of success to begin and will build a foundation for years to come!

Secondly, if you are seeking to create advertising campaigns stay away from Social Media Networks, for they are free to use and promote on by doing some clever simple marketing tricks, as mentioned earlier regarding Facebook and this is done by using trusted individuals and staff. Such tactics are not necessary with Twitter, as you can set up your Brand on this platform, for it is what it is a "News Feed Ticker" venue for press and product announcements and again free!

If I advertise or promote on the web that is going to cost me, it will only be through Google and Microsoft (Bing and Yahoo).

I would not necessarily go with text ads in my marketing strategy, as these can be lost in results and across web sites, where there is a great deal of text that Google or Microsoft promotes through. The other factor about text ads is, they can be very costly, as you end up in a bidding war for important related keywords.

Think about it in the days before the web, when we all use to advertise in related magazines and newspapers, they would be glossy and the advertisements were as big as possible subject to the budget allowed. Again this is speaking from experience, where even in the early 1980's I use to spend on average around £38,000 ($50,000) a month on advertising for the luxury sports goods business, which did pay off in the short, medium and long term.

So the most cost effective way of advertising and with the most impact, is to use what I describe as Brand Association and Awareness advertising campaigns. On the Google advertising program for example, the Google AdWords platform, you can select web site publications that you wish to advertise on. So if you are a sports business for example, it would be advantageous for you, if you promoted your products and brands on sports related web sites and online magazines.

The advertisement format I would opt for is display advertising. However, again very sadly, businesses and folk in marketing today, have become lazy and again taking the easy and superficial route of creating text based banner ads, instead of creating high quality display ads that portray the brand and image of the company well. These advertisement placements are also much cheaper and the impact is much greater especially after time, as the consumer user and reader becomes more acquainted with your brand, as they keep seeing your stunning advertisements promoting your great sporting products for example.

The great thing here also about this advertising, is you have a large range of different advertisement sizes you can take advantage of to reach your potential customers who are interested in sport from the very outset as a result of placement targeting!

Sizes most popular I would recommend to use are leader boards that are 300 x 250 pixels, 336 x 280 pixels, skyscrapers 600 x 120 pixels, 600 x 160 pixels and finally banners 728 x 90 pixels and 460 x 60 pixels.

These placement advertisements will be far more cost effective, but they will generate greater results in the short, medium and long term of your business and brand awareness success online.

Placement ads will have far greater impact!!!!

But remember from the very outset of advertising, design your placement ads so they give brand recognition, the same style and standards as seen in a glossy magazine and with the same time in design taken.

At this time in the marketing world there are many exciting things happening, where there is great opportunity to capitalize if you understand the environment.

Natural Law has an uncanny way of working through things for balance and this is in existence in everything we see, know and do. The smaller businesses today have been suffering to a great degree in recent years since the 2008 crash and the current changes underway will be more favourable to the small and medium business community.

You see with the emergence of more Social Media Networks today, it exposes the environment to dilution of these services that has been seen before with the Dot.Com bubble and the Television Broadcasting industry with the greater increase of TV Channels, resulting in the reduction of audience figures per channel.

I could see some years ago as Social Media Networks evolved, you would eventually see more Social Media Networks emerging, but becoming more specialized to cater for specific audiences and interests. We are now seeing this with the emergence of Social Media Networks for Entertainment and Music.

This is fascinating in many respects, as we are seeing the evolution of these services travel a full circle. When forums first emerged, eventually spin-offs from these saw the arrival of more specialist forums and this is now evident again with Social Media Networks, where part of the component element in the Social Media Network framework is forums in the form of posts etc.

So again, we can see from studying the history of our industry, can we accurately predict what is coming next. Earlier in the book, I mentioned the terminology "maintenance" and we are nearing this point now, where Social Media Networks will survive or die, as the dilution of these Social Media Network services become forever greater in number.

Now as a Business or Consumer user spending many hours, days, weeks and years on these Social Media Networks, this work or contributions will be lost as these Social Media Networks shutdown. This is another good reason why Social Media Networks can amount to nothing as just one example of wasted time and years. It is also another good example as to why the investment and time needs to be in your very own web site as a business, where you are in charge of your own destiny and simply using Social Media Networks as an opportunity to promote and direct users to your site all the while the entity exists.

Marketing in any form needs to be short, medium and long term, the name and brand of an organization needs to be subconsciously recorded and noted in every web user from your marketing skills.

Foundations and endurance are two key dimensions to build long term success and this is always required with most if not all tangible items manufactured and sold.

The name of any Business Brand is only as good as the products it sells and in marketing it does take time! This again is another element of consideration that appears to be forever lost today, as a result of an instant gratification society being created from the advancements in technology, believing everything should be instantly available. But this is not the case in the real World.

A VAT of high quality Malt Whiskey may take some 50 years to mature. Just because in a Virtual World such products are advertised online from an ecommerce store, does not mean that every aspect of the Brand and Business operation is quick and easy, for it never is in any worthwhile commercial operation.

Social Media Network marketing today is also having long lasting damaging effects on brands and companies from certain practices, as a result again of not understanding the environment and failing to appreciate that there are limitations when using technology.

When it comes to the consumer user sales, these are generated through emotions and brand iconic awareness. This is important to understand as you are dealing with a human being consisting of many emotional moods of change.

So unless you are absolutely mindless, you will appreciate that you cannot apply the same rules to emotional human beings and draw any comparisons to a PC with processing ability of artificial intelligence.

But the very sad truth is, Marketing Guru's and Social Media Network programming geeks believe they can by evolving intuitive data gathering for advertising.

Let me explain, you could make a phone call three times to the very same person in a day and at different times, but with the exact same conversation lines to the phone recipient and on each occasion the reply will be different in every case. This is for the simple fact that you are dealing with a Human Being and not a PC.

So this leads onto damaging the Brand and Business by offering countless marketing offers and gimmicks in the way of coupons etc.

For again as being human beings, the interpretation of such offers will vary between one user and another.

You may think OK that's fine if we only strike up say 30% in sales from such a campaign. But what you are missing is consideration for the other 70% who could be getting a negative experience and from such discontent to the point where they may block you on their email system and decide never to buy from you ever!

Coupons as like many gimmicks on the surface seem like a pretty good idea, but in most instances these offers offend rather than encourage.

I often get offers from Amazon after buying items, sometimes relating to free books as a result of my purchases, but when I use the offer, I am limited to a number of books and none of which suit me, or do I want. So now when these offers come through, I simply hit the delete button and so well done to the utterly mindless and stupid who believe they know about marketing!

Another great killer in potential customer relations is direct emailing, it is a protocol that has been around a long time and at the very beginning of the web it was agreed by the great minds that direct emailing was a "BIG" no, no and yet again the utterly mindless do it in marketing! For here again, from such stupidity, I and the rest of the World simply put you on an email block list and then that information is passed onto all the World's major players and where eventually you will find not only your emails on a black server list, but also your company web site. Well Done, Congratulations, you have just destroyed your Online Business now and for all time!

In marketing and especially today, you need to have trust and credibility for your Brand and Business. Again this does not come overnight and so if you set up a web site today and serve the community truthfully, free of breaking any ethical standards and protocols. After two years if you are lucky, MacAfee and Norton may decide for example, to list your Company Domain Name as a trusted web site, when appearing in search engine results, where you will see the little green icons (OK) of trust next to the listings.

If you want to be in Business with a great Brand on the World Wide Web and for the very long haul, smart moves start with really appreciating the environment, the protocols and understanding the limitations of Social Media Networking and utilizing such services as free marketing opportunities while they exist, but also retaining the rational degree of risk aversion and space between your Company and the Social Media Network by participating in such environments as an individual unless we are referring to Twitter or Google.

Good effective advertising comes from utilizing the big guns in the industry and using all their free tools available, so your advertising exploits are fruitful and these players being Google and Microsoft.

Legal Aspects

Today as consumers and even with businesses it appears the terminology and definition of the word and environment known as "Social Media" seems to give free license to cover up a multitude of sins!

However, the reality is surrounding Social Media in plain and simple terms, is its publishing!

What can come with the World of publishing are lawsuits both criminal and civil, dependent upon the severity of the case.

The likes of Facebook known as a Social Media Network site as far as I am concerned in legal terms, that such an entity is a publishing vehicle and is no different to the Huffington Post where both publish content.

At this time and perhaps it is fortunate for the users of Facebook and other Social Media Networks they retain a degree of ignorance, for the users are in effect contributing associates. Just as contributing associates or editors exist on the Huffington Post, Daily Mirror or the Sun Newspaper on or offline.

Facebooks' potential associate contributors amount to around 1 billion, as these are the figures currently being boasted by the number of users on Facebook today. The Huffington Post or the Daily Telegraph for example, may have a few hundred associate contributors. However, they are all within the arms-reach of the law if they breech it. This is the reason for having editors, to determine the accuracy and standard of the content being published. In Facebook terms this relates to the owners and senior managers responsible for this Social Media Network site publication for which it is!

Whist Facebook and other Social Media Networks are currently interpreted to be International Organizations on the World Wide Web without borders. These Companies are liable for the content material published in the States they are registered in as a Business.

Facebook's head office and main operations are in the United States of America and therefore accountable to the State's laws that exist.

Just because for example a Magazine or a Newspaper is sold internationally, does not exonerate the publisher regarding the content published inside and this are also the case surrounding Facebook and other Social Media Networks.

Therefore as like in Britain and the United States of America, where State Laws do exist and on Statute books to address the publishing of obscene material under the Obscenities Acts and Deformation Laws, to address the publishing of material that amounts to slander or deformation. Laws are also in place regarding the publishing of material deemed as criminal with regards to inciting or threats of violence.

Consumer users and Businesses need again to be especially careful surrounding material published on Social Media Networks as a great deal of material today is fraudulent and criminal.

As a consumer you simply cannot go around publishing offensive material or in more basic terms, slagging off someone you know or dislike as you are liable to prosecution under the law from some of the examples given above.

Just like a Business, it cannot publish material about a product or service that simply is not true, for such comments amount to fraud and can also be subject to breech of advertising standard laws.

The recent attempts to change or alter policy laws surrounding privacy is not necessarily required, for current laws only need to be tweaked and updated especially ones surrounding user registration on Social Media Network sites. So if material is published that is a National Security threat, or a fraud for example. Authorities can quickly track down the culprits and prosecute.

Any criminal activity, be it on the Street regarding a corner shop being robbed or online where a massive fraud has taken place, requires the co-operation of all community players as a business online or as a witness citizen in the Street and so the likes of Facebook are not immune.

Laws are in place today to address these many social ills. The Laws simply need to be actioned upon more and there also needs to be set in place a series of refresher courses to members of the Legal Justice System and Police Enforcement Authorities.

Facebook as a Social Media Network platform in recent years has been renowned for changing and altering policies to the point of saying they are constantly sailing close to the wind.

The changes very often invariably come down to users up in arms about their privacy and rights. But the harsh reality surrounding all these policy changes by Facebook relates to ownership of content, intellectual property disclaimers and navigating a path of legal litigation that allows such an organization to focus on the soul aim of making money!

Facebook as a Social Media Network Platform has no loyalty towards users, only the fear of losing them where they make less money from page impression exposure leading to more adverts being displayed to which they get paid.

If there was any noble cause as mentioned earlier surrounding Facebook, the organization would have never become a public company on the NASDAQ and joined the world of morally bankrupt corporate thugs, to which most of them are!

Again when you start to look at the legal aspects surrounding Facebook and others, there is no real certainty that these organizations will be in existence tomorrow and so you then have to consider all the hard work and content created by yourself over the years and where you stand surrounding your material that has been published on Facebook.

Again the harsh reality and real facts here is the legal policies have been carefully crafted so the material is no longer yours and they can do what they like with it!

Again as a business or as a user on and engaging with Social Media Networks, especially the likes of Facebook, such organizations have corridors of legal advisers and these folk are only working to one end and that is in the interests of Facebook their employer.

I have covered briefly the publishing of material content and the legal ramifications for producing such material. But then you have to also consider the legal ramifications and aspects surrounding intellectual property as a user or business.

I see many people across social networks sharing images or promotions in photographic form and often described as "infographics", the correct terminology being "data visualization" are again exposed to prosecution under copyright law.

You could be in a situation where as a user or business you take a random image and then dress it up with some form of promotional saying to benefit you or get a message out into the World, where you could be confronted with a lawsuit of using an image without permission that contravenes the law of intellectual property and copyright.

Let us say you have sold many products as a result of this campaign you have created with the image that belongs to another, in a legal position the victim being the owner of the image could very easily insist on a percentage of the income made from such a campaign.

Copyright breeches and passing off are very serious crimes and regarded as criminal acts, and as a deterrent such offences are often accompanied with a custodial sentence when found guilty.

I am particularly mindful and concerned about minors, for as a parent myself, there are many Mums and Dads who use Social Media Networks and do not understand the gravity or laws surrounding the publication of material or intellectual property laws.

The above actions taken by minors of using images or copying another's original content would not necessarily see action taken against the minors but in most cases the parents and sums in the way of legal costs and damages could run into several hundreds and thousands of dollars making a family homeless.

As I said towards the beginning of the book, "when entering the Lion's den be prepared to get bitten" and it is for these reasons above Social Media is not all it seems or appears to be!

The World of Social Media Networks is what it is!

What it is, is an environment of large Corporate Capitalist Empires today and when such entities come to be, they become servants of shareholders seeking bigger profits. They have no emotional ties, or consideration for others in fact they are sterile vassals and serve to the detriment of society.

The World Wide Web is one of the finest creations towards the end of the 20th century. Like any fish tank it is the environment and conditions that can threaten and kill the fish.

I do not understand how naïve society has become and especially business surrounding the lack of understanding concerning Social Media Networks.

As I near my 58th Birthday in November 2016, I have reached a point in my life where I consider risk aversion every day. Avoiding people, traffic, in fact anything that could become a negative or cause some form of disruption to my life and I apply the same deep thought in everything I create online and write.

Social Media Networks I fear today through lack of understanding are creating further burdens on society that will be very detrimental in the short and long term.

I truly hope the more Businesses use Social Media Networks for what they are and the limitations attached. Businesses need to start focusing more on their own web sites and this will then encourage more folk to hopefully explore beyond the borders of the likes of Facebook and others, for a more fulfilling and healthier lifestyle that will provide a more positive online experience.

Human Health

Throughout my 57 years plus of life at the time of writing this book, I knew our American Cousins were always over enthusiastic in all their endeavours and very often OTT to say the least. As a result many trends and characteristics of the American dream of gung-ho, go out and get, have now found their way into many other parts of Western Society.

The Social Media phenomenon has certainly become an environment to further demonstrate these characteristics of exhibitionist behaviour, especially with younger members of society, where the underlying theme is always portraying a positive experience to the World!

Thus far, I have often said in the book, Social Media is what it is and when it comes to the human condition, there needs to be a clear realization and understanding, that the World of Social Media is a virtual world and not the real world!

As mentioned in the previous Chapter Social Media are publishing networks and if it were a Newspaper or Magazine, there would be an editor in the equation determining the suitability of content. In other words, exercising some form of responsibility and accountability towards its readers and society.

However, as we know surrounding many Social Media Networks and especially Facebook, there appears to be no accountability or responsibility being exercised by Senior Management staff, as material continues to be published that is deeply disturbing surrounding Child Abuse and extremism.

Such material and images being published by Facebook and others can cause long term lasting damage to anyone and especially our younger folk. The great concern here also, relates to the human condition, where such virtual world content could affect the rational thinking, behaviour and decision making in a person's real world and life.

There are already signs of habitual cravings surrounding Social Media use, via the net from numerous device types today and especially mobile smart phones and tablet PC's. All of which are reliant on WiFi (wide area wireless computer networking) for connectivity to access the Social Media services on the World Wide Web.

Both mental and physical illness can come about from excessive use of Social Media Networks as the human body is a remarkable entity of human evolution over billions of years and within such a remarkable specie life form, the brain exists comprising of billions of neuron energy cells, sensors and nodes to transmit data.

To be able to see, hear, smell, feel and process the World around us including the connecting to the web relates to spectrum frequencies used for sight, WiFi, Microwaves, Radio Therapy etc.

So around us in this frenetic technological world that we live in today there exists tons of frequency waves of radioactive data that I suppose can best be described as atmospheric pollution.

The excessive use and very close proximity of these frequencies in the form of Wi-Fi with the use of Mobile smart phone devices close to your head can cause interference to the normal functionality of the human brain causing possibly fits, tumours, sight problems or nerve damage to the brain. Excessive exposure to radioactive waves on a continuous basis can also cause low sperm counts with reference to sexual reproduction.

The outdoors in relation to plant, animal and tree life with the inclusion of water environments, can and do help filter out a great deal of this atmospheric noise and pollution.

So regarding child and teenage development such excessive activity across Social Media Network sites and services may come with long lasting and very damaging health problems.

In our commercial world of capitalism today, the above concerns raised are not what any of these Corporate Monsters want you to read or hear and again, this demonstrates their lack moral character as enterprises regarding responsibility and accountability towards citizens and society.

Other great concerns regarding the health impact from Social Media is especially concerning and relevant to teenagers and minors, where they engage on Social Media and suddenly see a virtual world of fun, fun, fun!

Such sort of superficial exhibitionist behaviour of saying the blue sky is bluer and the yellow sun is more yellow and I look fab like this, or like that! Such superficial material content creates a distorted view in the virtual world of Social Media with regards to the real world at large, especially between teenagers and minors.

Such activity is very negative and non-productive towards the development of teenagers and minors. In fact based on the content published today on Social Media and especially by Facebook, there has been no real effort to introduce a mandatory verification age policy.

Reading this you may think I am a real square, but that is very far from the truth, as I really care about our future generations, as these young folk are burdened with the responsibility of trying to piece the World back together from our negligence today surrounding consumerism at the cost of all life and the Planet.

Nor am I delusional in any way, for as a Parent myself of 4 Sons and 1 Daughter, I am more than aware of what the little monkeys can and have got up too bless them over the years. None more so than with my Daughter and youngest years ago, when she hacked into the Schools Computers at just 8 years to upload her late School Project contribution to the School's web site.

For the record, she didn't get told off, I just laughed and gave her 10 out of 10, for her ingenuity and tenacity!

PC's, Monitors, Tablets and Mobile Smart Phones all emit radiation at varying levels. But the reality and fact is they do emit radiation! So the longer your loved ones are on such devices the greater the health implication risks.

Other health risks are more mental illness related and this is becoming of grave concern. These mental health conditions consist of depression, low self-esteem, suicide, self-harming, extremism and radicalization.

I have categorized extremism and radicalization under health issues, for in reality they are health issues created by an unhealthy environment in society and where Social Media is playing a significant damaging role that does not have to be the case.

It seems like many moons ago now but when forums started up and still continue today on Google and others, they were moderated and this simply meant that Social Media Networks, especially the likes of Facebook, should be employing more people to run their publishing service properly for which it is. Fact, material content generated and published, is publishing!

It is not necessarily the case for boys, but appearance is a big thing with girls and especially when they are teenagers and so for Companies especially modelling agencies to promote the female form appearing as some stick insect is deeply damaging and misleading.

It is especially damaging when young teenage girls are changing into young woman where the body form changes and very often to help counter these changes that also include bone structure changes, a degree of puppy fat is developed to ensure the bone structures can develop properly and can draw upon high fat proteins that help in bone structure development.

At such times in a teenager's life, they are very vulnerable and need support, as their world becomes turned upside down on a daily basis, due to the many hormone changes, bless them!

Therefore society and especially on Social Media needs to exercise a more collective and responsible approach, if we are to see a caring future generation emerging to ensure global peace and to maintain Earth so all life forms can co-exist and survive, finally seeing a World free of Corporate Industrialized pollution!

The advancements of technology today with Mobile Smart Phones regarding better photographic programs and device mechanisms is seeing a constant bombardment of more images, very often known and described today as selfies, which in many respects is a sad reflection of a more growing superficial society. The looks and appearance of Human Beings is becoming everything rather, than the really important gene code components in the form of human enlightenment, this being knowledge and intelligence.

When teenagers are especially seeing constantly glamourous images of young girls and women, they are very sadly and tragically naïve enough to believe this is how one should look in everyday life. This then leads to low self-esteem. With the addition of School bullying and name calling, can very often lead to children not eating properly and as a result having long term eating disorders. This could then lead to fatal consequences later on in life with heart, liver and kidney disease, unless they do manage to prevail and out-grow these very confusing and turbulent times as teenagers.

Additional serious matters of concern surrounding Social Media has been this worrying rise in public announcements surrounding acts of random killings and shootings especially on School and College Campuses in the United States of America and now other parts of Europe.

Many acts of self-harm, suicides and random killings is as a result of the environment society is creating, where greater pressures are being placed on young members of society feeling lost or trapped in a society framework of no hope or future.

Again we need to look at the bigger picture and understand the contradictions young members of society see, in the form of political corruption and failed public institutions that are there to serve and protect. But instead incumbents driven again by the capitalist mind set of self-interest and career advancement and at all costs and to hell with the rest. The same culture found across many Corporations including Social Media Networks, Hedge Funds and Banking Institutions.

Social Media in many respects is consigning Children and Teenagers to bedrooms and where they are not engaging face to face with parents, relatives or friends in the real world.

Such environments are not healthy for the development of any Child or teenager. Social Media in the superficial form as mentioned above amounts to web garbage, and certainly not a platform for greater enlightenment and learning as is the case with Wikipedia for example!

Other health issues from such an environment, is where Children and Teenagers become less mobile and lack healthy outdoor free exercise by participating in sports or other outdoor interests, where they begin to learn about the real world around them. What comes with that is another crisis in the form of obesity in young Children and Teenagers from a lack of exercise as mentioned and also loosing that important time up at a dinner table with the family discussing the world around them and eating full wholesome healthy food and not processed junk, or grabbing the odd sandwich, only to return back into ones bedroom again as a child or teenager.

The World Wide Web provides great opportunity for teenagers and children to become very pro-active to educate themselves about the World around them. Learn about hobbies, interests and pastimes where they can physically engage in tangible projects that will serve them well in later life. Some examples being finding out about healthy food recipes and learning to cook, tropical fish keeping, model making, dressmaking, car mechanics, fishing, horse riding, cycling, sailing, football, windsurfing, athletics, rugby, nature watch, pet care, conservation and much more.

Sitting in front of a PC, or holding a Smart Phone, looking at a Social Media Network page waiting for likes from a superficial post or image published is no life, or is it healthy for any member of society, especially Children and Teenagers developing.

In many respects, such behaviour is a lack of confidence and low self-esteem when someone is seeking likes in the form of popularity. This is the pre-cursor to mental health issues and the habit needs to be broken!

Online Cyber Bullying

It still seems only yesterday, where I had many great fond memories dating back to 1995 on the World Wide Web, a period that I described as "early hazy days" and the user population consisted of mainly students, academics and enthusiasts.

Since the commercialization of the World Wide Web, beginning in 1995, through to the present day, the community has increased on an epic scale. Where the whole of the World is connected and almost every home in Western Society especially, or where the web is accessed by mobile device users in their countless numbers now amounting to in excess of over a billion.

In the mix of inhabitants and web site venues to visit on the World Wide Web today, for education, services and products can be found every form of diversification, regarding people and content. Sadly, what comes with that is good and bad, or even worse still 'evil' by very disturbed people.

Cyber bullying has become a trait where it affects many people from all walks of life, be it celebrities through to School Children. The most significant victim numbers with regards to cyber bullying are found in chat rooms and across social networks. Regrettably, such events and offences are only going to increase, as more people become connected and tensions increase throughout societies, because of all the social and environmental challenges ahead.

So why does it happen and what are the causes?

Well, there can be many reasons for cyber bullying and it can relate to a broad spectrum of age groups. One of the greatest causes is jealousy! Celebrities suffer a considerable amount, from disturbed people, or others unhappy with their lot, as they say! Wanting to vent their anger and frustrations on others!

It is a sad reflection of our society, where jealousy can eat away at people. But what is so often forgot is that many deserving celebrities have trodden the boards as they say, for many years, if not decades, before they were discovered. Many celebrities before fame were desperate and homeless, living from hand to mouth, before they got their big break. But they never gave up and risked all, in pursuit of their passion and ambition.

Sadly, many who are spiteful and cruel, are cowards! For the life of me I don't know why, but really deeply resent other peoples successful lives. But what they forget is nothing is given to anyone on a plate. You have to go out and really graft, to achieve your ambitions and goals in life.

Between Children, cyber bullying again relates to jealousy. Where some children in a very unstable and troubled family environment, can become disturbed and angered, due to their circumstances and then take out their frustrations on others. Not every child can afford to have all the latest gadgets and gizmos. That is the reality of life and more Children have far less, than many perceive to be the case.

Many others especially adults, who behave in a cyber-bullying way, is as a result of themselves being troubled souls and in most cases where they need professional help. Mental illness is still not openly discussed enough today, but many in society suffer from such conditions, or even more serious health problems, including alcoholism, drug dependency and more.

To help yourself and them to avoid cyber bullying, when you do receive an offensive message that may emotionally hurt you for a brief moment, is to ignore it and not respond. You may be so angered yourself, you feel compelled to respond, but that is what the cyber bully wants. Instead of responding, be gracious enough to realize this person as the cyber bully has problems and in most cases, needs professional help for mental health issues.

The reason why a cyber-bully wants you to respond is so they drag you down to their disturbed and very sad level. For in most cases, cyber bullying is a way to say "Hey I Exist" for their lives can be so mundane, or inconsequential through a lack of confidence and insecurity, such actions of cyber bullying is their only form of communication in the world, where they can hide behind a computer screen or mobile device.

Cyber bullying is a frequent discussion today, especially with politicians, but their motives are more sinister. For if they can start legislating, they will be able silence social injustice and other short comings and be allowed to get away with even more than they do today, regarding their own self interests.

Cyber bullying can be a crime on a number of fronts. Anything written and placed on the web is publishing and there are Laws in place, regarding the obscenities act and deformation. There are also Laws, regarding threats to a person and a good lawyer in a Court can prove common assault, regarding the content of offensive cyber-bullying material. Authorities and legal bodies can also impose restriction orders and all such offences can be reported to Police authorities and should be!

Sadly, as I say jealousy is behind many such offences of cyber bullying. Throughout all walks of life there can be many jealous of others. Even when you are trying to help others, they can often try to bring you down as a result of problems they have with themselves.

Just recently, I had some abuse thrown at me by a lecturer in a University in England. Where he assumed I was a Conservative, or Republican on a topic, which is so far from the truth, as I regard myself as a citizen of the world and believe in social justice and human rights. After his abusive remarks, I merely replied "thank you for your gracious comments", the frustration of this person was not related to me, but his own circumstances and belief of injustice surrounding his wages and working conditions.

Sadly as a result of troubles within these people's lives, this can often be the catalyst and cause for their actions. So the most gracious and noblest thing to do is not to become a party, or participant to your cyber bully's troubled world of discontent or game.

Other signs of behaviour by Folk with trouble's, is when they try to correct someone on spelling, or some other insignificant thing. This again is a troubled soul and a form of control. It is a type of power, where they can correct you. Again it is a reflection on them, where they hold no prominence in society and hold no positions of trust or responsibility towards others in most cases. Again, it is a mental health condition of insecurity, where they again need professional medical help, to assist them suffering from low achievement, or esteem.

Cyber bullying can also appear in many guises. The recent events with terrorism and extremism, is where from a lack of education, folk become self-empowered when they have a gun. For they cannot articulate themselves, or hold their own in society, where they can challenge and carve out a peaceful future for themselves. In simple terms unable to face the complexities and realities of life as Men and Women.

Helping to avoid Cyber Bullying!

Learn risk aversion in your life, so always check who follows you, or who you choose to follow if on twitter for example. Take a look at their feeds and the same goes regarding Facebook and others. Check out their posts, before you engage.

Use the web as a positive for knowledge, services and products. When it comes to social networking, you need to be in control and be selective, to reduce the risk of abuse. You do not have to have lots of friends, or likes. You should know within yourself if you are a good person or not.

So finally to conclude, regarding cyber bullying by troubled souls. It is wise to not respond to these unfortunate folk who need professional help. By ignoring them in most cases, leads to the cyber bully moving on and leaving you alone in peace and is not seen necessarily as rejection!

Twitter

In recent days and weeks when writing this book there has been a great deal of debate surrounding the future of Twitter!

Well at this time and as I constantly warn folk how important it is to study history to determine the future. Twitter is one of those enterprises that has massive potential for at the end of the day it is the best form of an instant "Live Real Time News Feed" for any business, news, media, author, musician or user seeking to get out a product release or special announcement and a feed that can quickly trend and go viral.

Twitter News Feed Product Promotion Example: Picture by Alastair R Agutter

The Stock Market investors at this time cannot decide on Twitter, but then I am not surprised, as most of them are driven by money and know absolutely nothing about the geographical landscape of the World Wide Web or the gravity surrounding a turbulent and uncertain World around them!

Twitter regarding anyone making an announcement should be the number one venue to use first, as it is fast and simple, reaching the masses more than any other venue instantly, contrary to rumours and myths by others.

If you are in business, Twitter can be a great venue to develop brand awareness and especially if you configure the Meta Data on your products web pages that can grab the image and a summary of the product. This information will then also be displayed in the News Feed you post, as seen in the picture example above.

Throughout the day and weeks ahead, you can also promote products on a regular basis creating constant greater awareness of your brand and this will also quickly find and gather genuine followers that take an interest in your wares with a desire to buy.

You will come across new followers who claim to offer 1,000's of Twitter Followers for a fee, with figures ranging from as little as $5.00. But these promotions do not include real genuine followers and so these campaigns are not worth the paper they are written on as they say!

What these opportunists fail to realize with such promotions, is how desperate and negative they appear with such basement scam offers. I tend to ignore them and just despair, as it is a further reflection on folk in society generating nothing positive, or tangible, eventually such opportunists will find their accounts blocked and the details again placed on black server lists as spammers.

As an author these days, I am to a great degree limited to the number of News Feeds I can create on Twitter. But if I were back in business again, I would certainly make the most of Twitter to promote a catalogue of products with individual News announcement feeds and this activity in turn will help build the brand and increase Twitter followers, new potential customers.

The future of Twitter is without doubt secured, for I know colleagues at Microsoft will realize Twitter's full potential and will acquire such an entity to migrate and deploy such a fabulous service to their new Windows 10+ operating system desktop for an even more enjoyable and dynamic user experience.

At this time such a scenario above may seem impossible of happening, but be rest assured the wheels are already grinding in the background. As a member of the Microsoft Partner Research Panel a similar situation came about regarding the Yahoo Search engine and this opportunity was ceased upon from advice given by members and today the Microsoft Bing Search Engine service is a formidable player and only second to Google Search.

Facebook

It may be hard to believe but history tells me whilst Facebook is without doubt the biggest Social Media Network platform in the World at this time and boasting over 2 billion users, it is also the most vulnerable!

As a programmer and developer caught in the middle of the 'Browser Wars' in the mid to late 90's, between Netscape and Microsoft, it may of appeared unthinkable at the time regarding the outcome from when the 'Browser Wars' started, as Netscape commanded a massive 93% of all web users. Internet Explorer on the other hand, the Microsoft browser at the time when the 'Browser Wars' started, only retained a very small number of users in the 1's and 2's percent.

This is in very much respect the situation surrounding Facebook today and how Facebook the Social Media phenomenon is exposed just as Netscape was back in the mid to late 90's, but not to one rival being Microsoft as was the case then, but to two rivals namely Google and Microsoft.

Netscape's Achilles heel was as a result of not being in charge of its own destiny by having in place a 1st party environment of control. Whilst Netscape commanded 93% of the web's browser users, Microsoft held the key at the front end of technology by being the major operating system player of the day.

Microsoft simply went to PC manufacturers such as Hewlett Packard, Dell, Compaq and others advising them, if they carried the Netscape Browser on their OEM bundles that included an operating system, Microsoft would not supply the Windows Operating System to them.

Facebook is in the same situation today, Microsoft, Apple and Google hold front end control and power with operating systems and in addition they also have technology hardware today in the form of PC's, Tablets, Laptops and Smart Phones as part of their brand and product portfolio.

Any move by Facebook to enter into such an environment will mean war and both Google and Microsoft I am sure will join forces, as they have learned to live with each other now peacefully for around a decade.

Branding is also key here and let us all face it, who the hell would want to buy a Mobile, PC or operating system for that matter that had the name and brand of Facebook.

Today the image of Facebook is becoming one of distrust. Microsoft suffered with this to a degree back in the days of Windows XP, where I had a few frank and honest phone calls with Senior Managers regarding the trust and direction of the brand, especially when it came to the business community. Fortunately it was only a matter of a few weeks later, when a big marketing campaign was launched and commenced by Microsoft across television and many other media platforms, to regain trust in the brand and over time, Microsoft rebuilt trust with consumer and business users again and has continued to grow in stature.

You only have to look at the many policy changes of Facebook where it affects intellectual property and privacy, to quickly conclude Facebook is only driven by self-interest and profit. Hence the reason to float the organization, for if it were there for the community and promoting some noble cause, there would not have been any reason or motive to make obscene amounts of money for the owners and shareholders as a public company with the focus solely on profit!

Still today also as mentioned earlier and worth remembering again, Facebook are not interested in the type of content being published, for if they had one single fibre of morality in them, they would be hunting out and closing down Child Abuse and Extremist web sites on an industrial scale. I know at this point someone may say what about "freedom of Speech," well there is a great difference between freedom of speech and endangering the State, that amounts to treason where folk seek to murder and destroy a civil societies way of life!

The recent announcements by Zuckerberg to start giving all his wealth to Charity and good causes is a very cynical effort to find some form of respectability amidst all their deceit as a Capitalist thug. I say to Facebook pay your Taxes to the States that protect your Family and Staff every day!!!

The Facebook phenomenon has brought about gross negligence and complacency regarding the business community, where enterprise has been seduced by the possible potential of more customers and completely lost sight regarding the medium and long term damage to their brands. As a World respected News Media Group, the BBC promotes Facebook encouraging users to visit them on Facebook, moving them away from their very comprehensive web site and such policies are as a result of really bad advice by BBC incumbents and Marketing officials. For Facebook is guilty of publishing Child Abuse images and even guilty of secret paedophile rings and with the filth on the BBC surrounding Savile and his evil antics, it is clear there is no long term thought or strategy behind such decision making at the BBC.

I will be honest for I am not a hypocrite I have closed my Facebook account well over a year ago now, as I will not be associated with such a vile entity that does nothing to outlaw Child Abuse and Extremism.

So then you have to ask yourself as a Business or as a user, who the hell would want to be associated with Facebook!

Facebook accommodates many folk from all walks of society and so when in business specializing for example in one or two of these categories selling hats, bags, perfumes, jewellery, sporting goods etc. Only a very small percentage of users will exist on Facebook who could possibly be in the market for your products.

If you are in the luxury goods sector end, it is highly unlikely that very few if any sales at all will come from the likes of Facebook. Even if a celebrity or affluent user had a Facebook page by chance, I very much doubt they would boast such a fact if purchasing luxury brand items of value.

Quality brand and luxury goods sector users and potential customers would carry out the following exercise:-

1/. They would already know your brand and therefore go directly to your site or store.

2/. They would know your Domain Name and web site and therefore again go directly to the site or store.

3/. Search Google or Bing and locate the brands web site and then proceed directly from the results page using the related link.

Facebook in truth is what it is! The World of Marketing and Media have just looked at the numbers and read countless bullshit articles by folk who know nothing about Marketing, or the Landscape and History of Web Evolution.

Facebook while it exists can be used by trusted staff if need be to make posts to direct traffic to the Company Brand web site, therefore keeping a safe distance of non-association in any form and not wasting too much energy, time and money in the way of paying staff.

The situation regarding the BBC as a further example and the energy spent at the cost of Tax Payers money, to have staff creating posts and other material on Facebook, seems insane to say the least.

Especially in view of what I see looming on the horizon where something big is shaping up to happen that could determine Facebook's future and fate!

I really mean this, when folk invite me to Facebook offering a business service, I do think "come on please", it's like inviting me to a Car Boot Sale to buy a product or MacDonald's for a Business Lunch. No business can ever be taken seriously regarding such marketing gestures of stupidity. It will only be damaging to the brand in the short, medium and long term future of the business and its image!

Who are these people, get real!

Anytime spent on Facebook and other Social Media Network sites other than being very conservative with posts and promotions to direct traffic to your very own web site is a waste of content and money in staff terms.

Investment as mentioned in Marketing and Money should be directed to your very own web site, for every page created is another found on the major search engines such as Google and Bing for new and existing customers. Nothing is then lost and all the hard work will serve you well, by further building on the existing foundations created and not entering into any legal dispute at a later date over ownership of your material content and images. This is the current legal situation and position surrounding Facebook at this time and some other Social Media Network sites, who claim in the small print that any material published, becomes the intellectual property of the Social Media Network platform.

Other problems surrounding Facebook as irresponsible players, is where they turn a blind eye and still allow minors to use the service. Then minors become exposed to abuse in the form of paedophiles, cyber bullying and the list goes on to the point now, where we are seeing many mental health issues of self-harming, depression, and suicide to mention a few from low self-esteem and being taken in by a virtual world and not a real world!

So what do I see on the horizon regarding the future of Facebook. One thing I have learnt from studying history and especially surrounding the technology sector. However smart one believes they are they can never get the better of any State at the end of the day and especially not the United States of America Government? But Facebook if you will notice, are being very naïve to believe they can avoid paying Tax and continue to flout every law in the book surrounding the ethical and legal standards in publishing.

Nearly five decades ago, IBM (Big Blue) the World's biggest and most successful advanced technology company of their day, believed they could wriggle, twist, turn and be a law to themselves. Eventually the USA Government lost their patience and came down on IBM like a ton of bricks and literally smashed the Company to pieces and where today, whilst being one of the World's most successful and respected companies, pales in size and comparison to influence that it once held!

You see anyone who understands our industry and environment, would have noticed how Google and others are now toeing the line and volunteering past Tax contributions and the reason for this being especially after the recent stand-off between the USA Government and Apple surrounding Terrorism and user security, is the USA Government is shaping up again to exercise its power and the rule of Law. It therefore looks to be the case that Facebook are in their line of sight for bearing down on the Facebook Organization and prepared to take a hatchet to Facebook for all its Tax Avoidance, Tax Evasion and total disregard for the protection of minors and the continued violations regarding the publishing of illegal material content online, namely Child Abuse and Extremism!

The current set up of Facebook is where folk are working for them be it in business or as a consumer user and people need to wise up!

If a company or person were to ask you to spend on average between 30 to 40 hours a week working for nothing. Their reply and answer would be one of absolute amusement, such as take a long running jump off of the nearest pier!

But every business and user is working for nothing when they use Facebook, for every post you make, reply, like or visit to a friend's web site you get nothing. But Zuckerberg and his buddies at Facebook are laughing all the way to the bank. For every post, visit and comment made generates advertisement revenue from ad exposures that Facebook gets paid for and currently the owners and shareholders are racking in billions!

Now I am not a capitalist or a liberal or a socialist, I like to describe myself as a citizen of the World and so when I see such excesses of profit and greed, where these vile people are taking advantage

72

exploiting decent folk in society and seeing Children in the World starving every day, to me that's not on!

As more ex staff see through the cynical deception of Facebook with such skills they will set up something new on their own and the legacy of Facebook I am sure will be recorded and consigned to the history books as seen in the past.

It is not a question of if, but when, and be assured the storm clouds are now gathering on both sides of the Atlantic!

Google Plus

Google Plus in the World of Social Media has been steadily gathering traction now for a number of years, and will continue to steadily build to eventually challenge the likes of Facebook and others.

It does not indicate as is the case when Facebook was first launched an age trend. There are many folk from different age groups who use Google Plus and whilst some of the material published is by the utterly mindless in society the content quality is forever improving and for good reason.

Alphabet the parent company of Google and other brands they own has now for several years built in resilient steady robust development advancements.

This reflects on them today as a major player in the realms of AI (artificial intelligence) and where it can be clearly seen that there is a great appreciation for Sir Isaac Newton's Natural Law and especially surrounding the world of Quantum Mechanics, which teaches us to "evolve and Refine" and their advancements each day are more measured and considerate.

Therefore if you are a Google Plus member on Google's Social Media Network, you will notice from time to time changes being offered and considered with the co-operation of user feedback to attain a consensus of mutual appreciation and efficiency. Smart thinking!

The power of the Google Plus Social Media Network is such, that as a venue it works in concert with their flag ship search engine service that is the envy of the World and so when you post on Google Plus as a Social Media service, within a matter of minutes this information can be found in the search engine results for Google Search Engine users to find.

If you are a business developing a brand and marketing products this can literally be music to your ears!

To demonstrate my point in this section of the book are the two following images, where I have posted a product on the Google+ Social Media Network, and then in the second image, you can see the Google+ Social Media Network post appearing in the Google Search Engine results, a short time afterwards!

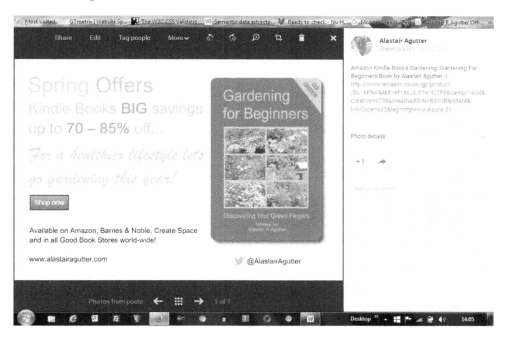

Google+ Image One Posting a Product Feed: Picture by Alastair R Agutter

The Google+ Social Media Platform is an evolving project on Google and so some investment can be made by your business, as it is evident that Google's long term objective is to counter the

Facebook emergence that has had some impact on their strong and commanding position as the advertising market leader.

Again the smart move involves the posting of product news and information aimed towards your own web site. Not only for gaining more customers and sales but also gaining greater popularity use in the Google Search Engine results increasing your ranking within the Google hierarchical measurement metrics system and algorithms.

The World of the Web and Technology can never be taken at face value as there are some really seriously clever folk in the industry who do not think one dimensionally and so there is very often a number of factors and facets surrounding a technology environment. This is the case and a prime example surrounding Social Media and Search Engine Technology.

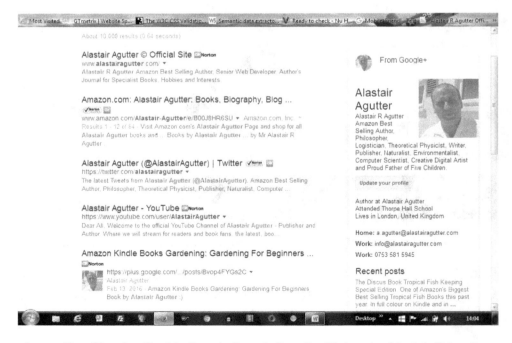

Image Two Showing Post in Google Search Results: Picture by Alastair R Agutter

The Google+ Social Media service are also introducing and providing technologies so clubs and groups can be formed of interest to folk. This is another smart move as it helps to find potential customers who share an interest in your products.

A good example to this would be if you owned a business selling fishing flies and materials. Where from the power of Google+ it would make sense to either set up, or track down clubs and groups that tied Flies or are into Fly Fishing as a potential product captive audience!

YouTube

YouTube today is a major player involved and associated with the World of Social Media and becoming a forever more popular venue for many forms of rich media information and entertainment with massive potential to get out the message surrounding a product or brand especially.

But YouTube today is also becoming a popular venue for educational tutorials and also rich media reference guide presentations for hobbies, interests and pastimes covering many topics and fields of interest.

As a business there is great opportunity on YouTube and if we just take Jamie Oliver as one fine example where he provides video production broadcasts on recipes to help promote his web site, books and restaurants. He is testament to the success that can be achieved by using the power of Social Media Networking and Jamie has got it right! For every post and feed he makes across Social Networks are targeted towards his own web site.

As an Author myself I do know what it takes to sell and market books and with the help of my fabulous publishers and distributors at Amazon and also my loyal book sellers and book store retailers around the World.

The aid of Social Media in the right way as covered in this book and especially the power of rich media here on YouTube can be the icing on the cake when it comes to brand awareness and product marketing!

I take my hat off to Jamie Oliver, for I know how hard he works and for his efforts has reaped the rewards with many Best Selling books and over 10 million sold world-wide and the 2nd most successful author after J. K. Rowling of the Harry Potter series of books and film in Great Britain!

Best Sellers do not come easy, it takes a great deal of hard graft as I say and clever marketing, but with a structured plan and all directed to your own main web site and using Social Media Networks as part of the branches in your marketing plan and where your web site is front and centre as the hub and by applying such methods great success will come!

Today with the continued advancements in Broadband and WiFi to successfully deliver rich media content, YouTube as a Media Platform is a must, if the skills and resources are in place!

As a Company marketing your brand on YouTube, the work needs to be polished, but on tutorials and guides, presentations can be more down to earth and have a human face to the work so audiences can engage, Jamie Oliver is a good example and worth a watch on YouTube!

For my sins I was one of the very first in Britain to start designing and programming Rich Media with RealNetworks as a Partner Producer in the mid to late 90's and in those days, I had to battle with 28k and 56k modem connectivity and in relation to today's connectivity as a comparison, it can be best described as at a snail's pace.

But from the very early outset of the commercial web as I call it, rich media was always the Holy Grail in electronic media and today we can all start that journey with fabulous free program support from friends and colleagues at Microsoft with Windows Live Movie Maker, that is a fabulous program to develop rich media advertisements, book and film trailer promotions, short films, media programmes for cookery, hobbies, interests, tutorials, guides and much more!

As a result of YouTube and its power, the platform has the ability to change folk's fortunes and lives. It can also be the answer to brand awareness and product launches.

YouTube was in fact the venue that gave the great artist Adele her first break, when she posted her first song on YouTube and where a large recording and record label saw her work!

If you use the Microsoft Windows Live Movie Maker program, you can produce and save your productions in a number of formats including Mp4 and upload these tutorials, short promotions, or product launches onto your own web site as a further attraction for your web site venue visitors and customers.

Again YouTube today is a maturing and evolving platform with support of parent organization Google and so any investment and time made towards YouTube will be a long term brand awareness investment.

The YouTube Platform will only continue to improve and evolve just like the Google+ Social Media Network site as Google the parent organization will continue to meet demand and expectations of its Google Search users where the benchmark standard is quality in relation to search results.

Such services as YouTube and Google+ further enhance the Google portfolio of services and applications for their users, and any business association with Google is a smart move in marketing for developing your brand and products.

Linked-in

Linked-in as a Social Media Network is more designed towards the business community and when it was first launched in 2003, there was a great deal of hype in the Business Media world by players such as CNBC.

But even after 13 years the Business Social Media platform is still seeking out answers regarding the long term viability of the project.

First-hand experience tells me when you become focused on a specific area such as business the large piece of the cake becomes forever smaller with reference to audience base interest.

In an informative World this is a good thing as like in hobbies and interests where such topics are covered in more detail such entities help evolve the advancement of the human story and journey.

However in the commercial world of business and especially regarding public companies the focus is more on money and shareholder profit!

Towards the end of last year the Linked-in organization asked my advice on how they could locate and improve the quality and availability of computer programming skill set technicians and developers in the industry and what it took to be successful in these sectors.

As always my advice was frank and truthful and the words to best describe such an environment requires great dedication and endurance as pointed out by the President, Barack Obama, when asked by Bear Grylls about the human condition for success in the most powerful office in the World. Where the President replied and said "to make a good leader is not the most intelligent man or the

81

most physically strong, but someone who is smart and has endurance." These I believe are the qualities required in Computing and the Sciences, for I have come across many who are highly intelligent but lack the endurance for any business operation that is never a sprint but a marathon.

The reason such questions were being asked by Linked-in is for the fact that they know there is much more to be done to make Linked-in a very popular and dynamic business Social Media Network Platform service.

One of Linked-in's biggest mistakes to date is drawing comparisons to other Social Media Network entity successes and trying to apply similar services and gimmicks as I call them to their model. Such novelties serve no place in a business environment, not even on a Business Social Media Network and this again is why in Business you have to be very careful who you associate yourselves with to ensure you protect the company brand.

Linked-in is what it is!

Linked-in is a Social Media Network in Business and therefore the audience base will be far lower in number and the evolution and expansion of the brand will be far slower.

Initially like any new service, there will always be a case where there will be an initial sign up to a service (where fools rush in). But the more mindful and strategic will sit and wait it out and sometimes for a considerable time, and in some instances, taking many years before a serious player will sign up and engage in a service, if they believe there is some synergy and benefit to them.

Some of the most recent feature additions to the Linked-in service, reflects the desperate need to make money and see a return. But the secret to any great marketing and development of a brand or service is always to keep it simple (kiss).

Some of the greatest advertisements of all time promoting a great brand, has always derived by keeping it clean as I say! These were very highly polished advertisements promoting a product or brand.

The introduction of more features to the Linked-in service is making it look messy and over complicated when navigating the service. It is clear that whoever is responsible in the design architecture of the Linked-in Social Media Network Platform, they are clueless about marketing or business!

Linked-in needs to make this service more highly polished in design and simple, easy to navigate. Not every business owner or staff member is a computer whizz and so making the service complicated in navigation which it is, will discourage business owners and staff from tracking down and hunting out new talent for their businesses.

I have noticed linked-in are now mailing out a great many key position offers to members and this is another sign of trying to establish its value and use in the community.

I registered with Linked-in for the only reason being, it was a case of having too. It provides an opportunity to publish background experience, skills and vision.

Regarding views, opinions and posts their mechanism is more geared to feature posts that benefit them in the way of name association of household or celebrity names in the business industry.

If you have a product or brand you wish to promote with a post, it will only appear for a brief time before it is relegated so a more known personality or company is featured.

Like Facebook Linked-in is more focused on money and profit for themselves, rather than focusing on the development of the service that could become substantial over time and serve the business community, but very sadly, this a secondary consideration. History tells us that any entity or idea with such a mind-set is never sustainable long term.

Today we still see the Stock Markets in business seen as the greatest success in capitalism. But the reality is when you look beyond the ignorant masses that believe such tosh. These institutions have been systematically bailed out and propped up since their inception and especially through the past century especially.

Some may question such a claim, but the reality is the programme of Quantitative Easing most recently by State Banks such as the Bank of England and the Federal Reserve, amounted to the printing of money by Governments to bail out banks and such money was then lent to existing Corporate Giants they already had heavy investing and lending with! The real economy surrounding rapid employment, advancements and growth is always from Small and Medium enterprises, but sadly they have always remained as a poor relative to the social elite club of Corporate Capitalism and Corrupt Banking!

Linked-in very sadly buys into the quick and easy money culture that is now threatening all of society from weak Governance of States failing to bring into line over decades these Capitalist thugs or Corporate Empires as they are described, found across banking, finance and the services sector and where none of them actually produce any tangible products.

Linked-in also offers a premium service to members, but again when these offers and promotions are viewed by the more informed, again it indicates a position of desperation and where the reaction is a despairing sigh just before you press the delete button on your PC or Laptop to remove the message!

If Linked-in can offer a better service to users, well then they should offer the better service! The idea of charging for such a service is a basement level concept that will turn new members and users off!

Linked-in as I say is more focused on "what's in it for them" and such values in business always spell failure. Great businesses succeed from an idea transformed into a brand and product to change and make a better world for all!

My visit to the Linked-in Business Social Media Platform today and based on my valuable time is occasional, and only for updating the profile page to add a new book release for example. Or on some occasions to post a very important article that relates to the interest of all internationally.

The only other occasion to visit Linked-in is when someone seeks to connect, but here I am very selective and will always give someone a helping hand starting out or highly respected in the community who share my values, but not someone seeking to connect for the sake of it, or who is engaged in some morally bankrupt sector of the property sector for example. For such association can again damage your brand and very sadly many in business fail to consider such factors.

Another dangerous area in Social Media and especially in business is political views. Fortunately for myself I tell it how it is and know how damaging it can be when I express my views, but I am never going to fall off of the path of truth and sincerity, especially when it relates to the health of humanity and all miracles of evolution we have come to love and know!

But as a business expressing a political view or opinion, again it can damage your brand, for you have to consider your potential customer base have different political views and opinions.

Always remember, any posts or feeds you publish need to be targeted towards your web site and remember also to be conservative in your time and energy when using Linked-in and other Social Media Networks to benefit you not them!

Linked-in does fare well in the Google Search Results and so it does deserve a small amount of your time and to ensure the profile is current, especially regarding brands and products if in business.

Linked-in offers a project section on the profile pages and I would use these to feature your different brands and again with links to your own web site. For the more links into your web site, this increases your ranking importance on Google and they will place you higher in the search engine rankings and begin to spider and data mine your web site for new content more frequently.

As I have mentioned before, the web and the artificial intelligence aspect is not one dimensional and like Natural Law and Quantum Mechanics all is related and connected. So actions and decisions made on one Social Media Platform may have an impact in other areas of the grand scheme of things when it comes to your business and brand development.

Yes Social Media can be a minefield and yes it can be time confusing and a waste of energy in certain areas and even serve as a negative as pointed out in relation to Facebook.

I also know millions of sites offer links to Facebook and other Social Media sites today, but in truth this is more based on ignorance rather than intelligence!

Think about it, why the hell you would want to drive customers onto another web site, when you have them on your own in the hope they may buy a product or service.

The truthful answer is it makes no sense and it's that old adage of the blind leading the blind!

The others

Today more than at any time there are more Social Media Network sites and services being opened. Again it is history repeating itself as it was a similar environment in the mid to late 90's surrounding the explosion of Forums online.

Today we have Pinterest, What's App, Instagram, Tumblr and the list goes on!

By engaging in many of these Social Media Networks, it can become very time consuming and costly if you have to pay staff.

Again it is a question of protecting the brand and understanding your market, so the more diverse social media becomes the more selective you have to be with regards where you promote your brand and business online!

If you are specialists in high quality Gardening Equipment for example, posts on Instagram is both a waste of time and money and so you will need to target more your potential customers and new users.

What is happening, as a result of these new Social Media Networks emerging is dilution again and this is why it is important to focus and invest in your own web site.

For as these Social Media Networks come and go, which they will in the coming years, by investing your time in your web site promoting your brand and products will always remain a constant in the web community and will therefore continue to be a friend to Google and Bing, who are always seeking to improve and maintain a great web user search experience by delivering accurate quality search results!

Some business brands and products can adopt relationships with new and emerging Social Media Networks as well as existing ones surrounding women's fashion and make up for example. Where visual impact can often sell products, but again with the intention of any marketing in the form regarding posts, must always be directed from the Social Media Networks to your web site, so users and customers can acquire the products and also where they can become immersed in the brand's image and culture, good examples being Cartier and Gucci.

Weaponization of Social Media

Today sadly, and this has been evolving for a few years now, is the Weaponization of Social Media, where it can be used to influence users, none more so than in the world of politics.

Today with the measurements and algorithms constantly gathering information, attackers can easily establish their audience base say for the Labour Party Voters in Britain, and then tailor a massive detrimental set of advertising campaigns that look like news for example and about the candidate, or party, to encourage a swing to the other parties involved.

Years ago a lot of this was carried out in the United States and the Nixon era was testament to that and the Watergate scandal. In those days it was mainly door knocking, mail outs, adverts on TV and letters. The term in the industry was known as "Rat Fucking" to attack and bring down another opponent.

Such power today can in fact bring down Governments. The Arab Spring was as a result of the power of Social Media where oppressed Folk in other parts of the world saw for the first time via a smart phone how others were living, and collectively decided they no longer wanted to live in poverty and misery. But live how others do around the world and especially in Western Society, leading to social unrest and conflict, the most tragic of these being to date Syria.

During the Cold War, data was always stolen and acquired with the use of micro film and the use of couriers (agents), travelling from one Country to another.

But today with social media, you just need a few talented hackers, and some money to unleash hell across social networks.

Therefore it is imperative that users should never be complacent. Especially businesses, for their brands could easily being used in a name association capacity by an alien power in a more covert operation.

As a brand also, you need to ensure your own advertisements do not become displayed in such hostile environments of fake media and abuse that leads to long-term damage to an established, or new emerging brand.

Conclusions

As I say to friends regarding any of my books to help the community, if I write about the subjects as a form of reference, well then the information is available.

I hope this book will help and not necessarily in the way you may of thought. But I do know the information is extremely valuable and will help to apply a great deal more thought into proceedings surrounding Social Media Networks that will come and go!

When we engage on the World Wide Web we are communicating with the World and all its diversity. Within such a pool can be found the most intelligent to the most profound and as such, greater depth of thought and understanding must be applied.

As we travel our life's journey, we are always in search of answers and very often the road or path we take can lead to some interesting conclusions.

I like to describe our journey as a process of learning for greater enlightenment and then from such understanding you will reach a point in your life when you realise that the "Answer has no Answer."

Today many of my views, opinions and sentiments may not appear to be relevant or apparent at this time in your life's journey, but there will come a time when they do become relevant and all make sense.

On the following pages are some useful links that will help you on your journey and especially regarding the investment required in developing your own web site.

Nearly a year ago to the day, my colleagues and friends at Google changed their search engine rankings metrics and algorithms to reward web sites that were PC and Mobile friendly, this relates to the realms of RWD (responsive web design) where web site pages can alter dimension to meet the demands of the device user, be it through a PC, Laptop, Tablet or Smart Phone etc.

A very special and close friend who has lectured in the Gandhi University in India once said "with change comes opportunity" and so any changes and decisions you have to make today comes with it opportunity. Thank You!

Sincere Best Wishes,

Alastair R Agutter

Author ☺

Useful Links

Please find the following useful links, that I hope will be of great help and value, also help you when investing in your own web site, to develop your brand and products.

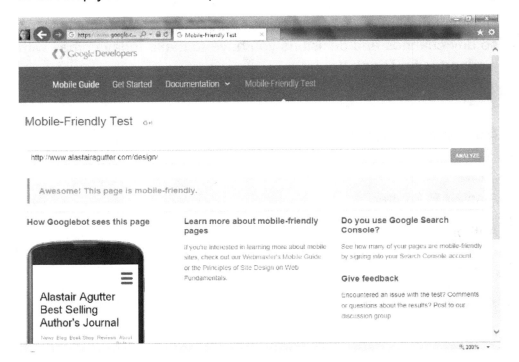

1/. Is your web site Google Mobile Friendly:

https://www.google.com/webmasters/tools/mobile-friendly/

2/. Is your web site Fast:

https://gtmetrix.com/

3/. Does your web site Cascading Style Sheets comply:

https://jigsaw.w3.org/css-validator/

4/. Does your web site HTML Web pages comply:

https://validator.w3.org/nu/

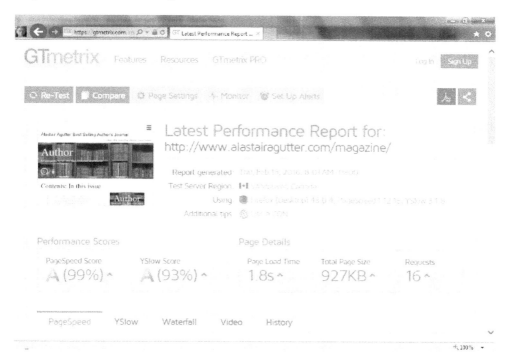

5/. Does your web site provide web semantic information for search engine Data Mining?

https://www.w3.org/2003/12/semantic-extractor.html

6/. Alastair Agutter Author's Journal

https://www.alastairagutter.com/

7/. Google Developers

https://developers.google.com/

8/. Google Webmaster Tools

https://www.google.com/webmasters/tools/

9/. Google Adwords

https://www.google.co.uk/adwords/

10/. W3C Html 5.0

https://www.w3.org/TR/html5/

11/. Alastair Agutter (Author) Printed and Digital Books

https://www.alastairagutter.com/

12/. Jamie Oliver Web Site Example

http://www.jamieoliver.com/

13/. Cartier Web Site Example

http://www.cartier.co.uk/

14/. Gucci Web Site Example

www.gucci.com

15/. Google Search Engine

https://www.google.com

16/. Microsoft Bing Search Engine

https://www.bing.com/

17/. Wikipedia Social Media

https://en.wikipedia.org/wiki/Social_media

18/. Rolex Web Site Example

http://www.rolex.com

19/. Wimbledon Web Site Example

http://www.wimbledon.com/index.html

20/. BBC Web Wise

http://www.bbc.co.uk/webwise/

20/. Alastair Agutter Amazon

http://amazon.com/author/alastairagutter

21/. Alastair Agutter @Twitter

https://twitter.com/AlastairAgutter

22/. Alastair Agutter Blog

http://www.alastairagutter.com/wordpress/

23/. Alastair Agutter Google

https://plus.google.com/+AlastairAgutterPublisher/?rel=author

24/. Alastair Agutter RSS Feeds

http://www.alastairagutter.com/rss/news.xml

25/. Adele's Web Site Example

http://adele.com/

26/. Microsoft for Windows Live Movie Maker

http://windows.microsoft.com/en-gb/windows/movie-maker

Related Author Publications

I hope these following publications may be of additional help or of interest for my Readers sharing an interest in Social Media, Web Technical Authoring, Programming, Web Design, HTML 5.0, CSS 3.0, RSS 2.0+, Web Optimization and more.

At the time of writing this book, all the following titles have already been published or due to be released. Thank You!

1/ Getting Inside Google's Head Book

2/. Creating the New Internet Super Highway

The Author's Books are available world-wide in Print and on Digital. Thank You!

https://www.alastairagutter.com

Acknowledgements

Special thanks to all my fabulous Readers acquiring this book dedicated to you in the interests of serving the wider community to shape a better world for all tomorrow. Thank You!

Special thanks also to friends and colleagues in the technology community who continue to serve humanity with measured advancements by respecting the founding principles of Sir Isaac Newton's Natural Law.

Quotation:

"We all need to understand and appreciate the role and importance of technology, where it is there to assist, not to make us dependent."

~ Alastair R Agutter